# Introduction

Here we are at the second half of the book of Joshua. The Jordan has already been parted, allowing the Israelites to cross into the land they've spent the last 400 years longing for and the last 40 years staring at. They have already marched around Jericho for a week, before blasting on their horns so the walls came tumbling down. Achan's sin has been uncovered and dealt with, Aii has been destroyed, and all but one of the great battles have been fought, including the one where God made the sun stand still in the sky for a whole extra day.

At first glance, it looks like all the good stuff is over and only the long chapters of tribal allotments, complete with hard-to-pronounce towns and cities, are left. That was the general response I received when talking to friends and family about this study guide. One person even went so far as to say, 'There is nothing of relevance to us today in that half of the book.' A bold statement indeed! And one that couldn't be more mistaken. Let's not forget that 'All Scripture is God-breathed and is useful for teaching, rebuking, correcting and training in righteousness', as Paul stated in 2 Timothy 3:16. He wasn't just talking about the exciting or well-known bits of the Bible, but *all* Scripture, the tribal allotments included.

That said, the land distribution is not all we have left. We have the closing battle of Joshua's campaign, fought against their greatest enemy yet: Jabin, the king of Hazor, which was one of the most populous and powerful cities in the world at the time. We have two stories of Caleb's wholehearted devotion to God at the age of 85. We find out what happened to the Levites, the tribe who received no land but whose inheritance was God Himself. We learn about how building an altar nearly led to a civil war, and we have Joshua's last

two speeches, calling the people to commit themselves to serving the Lord and driving the Canaanites from the land. Pretty exciting stuff! And, as Paul wrote in his first letter to the Corinthians, 'These things happened to [the Israelites] as examples and were written down as warnings for us' (1 Cor. 10:11). This isn't just history; it's valuable information for us in our walk with God.

It isn't a surprise then, that the focus of this half of Joshua is on service to God. The first half had mainly been about getting into the Promised Land and wiping out the people already living there. (This second item causes something of a problem for many Christians who find the idea of our loving, merciful Father commanding, and even assisting, the wholesale genocide of thousands of people not only distasteful but even possibly contradictory to the rest of Scripture – and this is something we will be considering and hopefully dealing with as we work through these sessions.) But now that the campaign is almost over and the Israelites are about to divide up the land and start settling into their new homes, the time of expectation and excitement is giving way to what we might call normal, everyday life – where service to God has a tendency to drift into the background. Beforehand, they were desperate, wholly reliant on God providing and interceding for them. Now, they can kick back, enjoy their lovely new land and its produce, and focus on their families and on life in general. Just like today, when life is ticking along nicely and one day merges into the next, it is all too easy to forget there is a God who has called us to serve Him – to work with Him, to get to know Him, to grow in love for Him. Serving God is not only something that happens on a Sunday, or when life is tough and when things aren't going our way. Serving God is something that encompasses every waking moment of our lives... or at least that's what we're going to see in this book. And so we are presented with a choice every day: who will we serve?

# COVER TO COVER

BIBLE **STUDY**

7 SESSIONS FOR SMALL GROUP
AND PERSONAL USE

# Joshua 11–24

## CALLED TO SERVICE

**CWR**

Phin Hall

Published 2019 by CWR, Waverley Abbey House, Waverley Lane, Farnham, Surrey GU9 8EP, UK. CWR is a Registered Charity – Number 294387 and a Limited Company registered in England – Registration Number 1990308.

The right of Phin Hall to be identified as the author of this work has been asserted by him in accordance with the Copyright, Designs and Patents Act 1988 sections 77 and 78.

For a list of National Distributors, visit cwr.org.uk/distributors

Scripture references are taken from the Holy Bible: New International Version® Anglicised, NIV® Copyright © 1979, 1984, 2011 by Biblica, Inc ® Used by permission, All rights reserved worldwide.

Concept development, editing, design and production by CWR.

Every effort has been made to ensure that this book contains the correct permissions and references, but if anything has been inadvertently overlooked the Publisher will be pleased to make the necessary arrangements at the first opportunity. Please contact the Publisher directly.

Cover image: Adobe Stock

Printed in the UK by Linney

ISBN: 978-1-78951-138-3

# Contents

As we voyage through these weekly studies, we will discover
how serving God requires a daily choice to be totally dependent
on Him, following Him devotedly and wholeheartedly with all
our time, energy and resources, influencing similar service
in others. We will explore how our actions are shaped by our
faith, and how our unity as God's people is vital if we are to
serve Him effectively.

You will get the most out of these sessions if you take the time
to read through the complete passage assigned to each one
before you start working through the discussion starters.
Some of these passages are fairly long, but be encouraged:
they really are worth the effort. My prayer is that, as you use
this study guide, and work your way through this challenging
second half of the book of Joshua, you will discover what it
means to be part of the people of God, and so grow together in
your love and service of Him.

WEEK ONE

# The campaign's conclusion

## Opening Icebreaker

Nobody can resist the challenge to throw a screwed-up paper ball into a bin! Find out who thinks they are the best thrower and pit them against the rest of group (as a single team) to see who can get the most paper balls into a bin in 30 seconds (see Leader's Notes).

## Bible Readings

- Joshua 11–12 (if short of time, read 11:12–23)
- Genesis 15:16
- Daniel 5:20
- 2 Corinthians 12:7–10
- Acts 2:42–47
- John 15:1–5

**Key verse:** Joshua 11:6

**Focus:** Serving God requires total dependence on Him.

## Opening Our Eyes

As we pick up the thread in chapter 11, Joshua and the Israelites have just faced the full might of the five kings in the south – an enemy so vast that God made the sun stop in the sky for an extra day to give the Israelites time to defeat them and take their cities. Now, Joshua turns his attention to the northern inhabitants where Jabin has gathered his allies and is preparing to fight... which seems crazy! They must have seen the sun stop and heard about the Israelites' triumph against the southern inhabitants. Why wouldn't Jabin try to make peace with them instead, like the Gibeonites did?

We find the answer in Joshua 11:20: 'it was the LORD himself who hardened their [the Canaanites'] hearts to wage war against Israel, so that he might destroy them totally'. The idea of God hardening hearts tends not to sit well with us today. After all, we've placed our hope in God's abundant grace and mercy. Why is He so ungracious towards the Canaanites? We will be tackling this question in more depth in Week Six, but for now let's remember that, back in Genesis 15:16, God gave them over four hundred years to change their ways, but they didn't. Even so, the phrase 'hardened their hearts' does not necessarily imply that God turned them against the Israelites, rather that He strengthened their resolve. Ultimately, they hardened their own hearts first. And so Jabin gathers up 'a huge army, as numerous as the sand on the seashore' (Josh. 11:4) – far larger even than the army Joshua faced in the south. What miracle will it take to overcome them? How long will the sun have to stand still *this* time? Amazingly, the whole thing is over in a single sentence: 'Joshua and his whole army came against them... and the LORD gave them into the hand of Israel' (Josh. 11:7–8).

Done.

Having chased the Canaanites down, slaughtered them and taken their cities, they then hamstring the horses. This last detail might seem a curious thing to point out – a seemingly insignificant action – but it was a specific command from the Lord, and it tells us something about the Israelites and what they have learned since leaving Egypt. Though they witnessed the ten plagues, the parting of the Red Sea, and saw the fire and smoke at Mount Sinai, they didn't trust Him, going so far as to build a golden calf to worship instead of God. They didn't trust Him to protect them from Pharaoh. They didn't trust Him to feed and water them. And they didn't trust Him to give them the land, due to the giants that were living there. The result was their 40-year sojourn in the desert.

Maybe it was the daily reliance on manna to keep them alive or the many victories God has given them, but the Israelites have learned, at least in part, to trust God. So rather than keep the horses and their chariots – which would have been a massive advantage against any foe and therefore something to put their trust in – they destroy the chariots and hamstring the horses, rendering them useless for warfare. This is echoed in Deuteronomy 17:16, where God told them that their future kings were not to 'acquire great numbers of horses' because they were to rely on God alone. It's an unpleasant thing to do to the poor animals, but the Israelites have demonstrated their reliance on God, rather than in any worldly strength.

Chapter 12 lists the 31 kings they have beaten and, with this, Joshua's campaign to take the land is over. It's time for the settlement to begin.

## Discussion Starters

1. What struck you most as you read through these final chapters of the Israelite campaign to take the Promised Land?

2. Daniel 5:20 tells us that hardening our hearts is the result of pride. How would you define 'pride'?

3. Read 2 Corinthians 12:7–10. Paul was at his strongest when he had nothing left but reliance on God. How might our weaknesses make us stronger in God?

4. We each have areas of weakness – whether physical, mental or spiritual – some may seem insurmountable. How is it possible to turn such weaknesses into strength in God?

**5.** Which of your strengths might cause you to be less reliant on God?

_____

_____

_____

_____

**6.** In John 15:5, Jesus suggests we are reliant on God for everything – every act, every word, every decision. But how far should we take our dependence on God? Are there things we can get on with without seeking His guidance and strength?

_____

_____

_____

_____

**7.** Consider how the Early Church in Acts 2:42–47 relied on one another, and discuss ways in which this is or isn't lived out in your own church community.

_____

_____

_____

_____

## Personal Application

Pride is the belief that we do not need God. Just think about that for a moment. Surely the most ridiculous belief imaginable, and yet quite possibly the most popular attitude towards God throughout human history. The promotion of independence and self-reliance battles with the reality that we are all dependent on God for everything – every sip of water, every morsel of food and every breath of air. Hebrews 1:3 talks of Jesus 'sustaining all things by his powerful word'. Without His continuous intervention, the whole of creation would cease to be… and yet we still believe we don't *really* need Him. We still harden our hearts, even if only in part, trusting in our own strengths.

Humility is the opposite of pride – it is the belief that we need God, and that we need the help and support of one another. Have a read of John 15:1–5 and take the time to meditate on Jesus's words of humility, dependence and resting in God's glorious provision.

## Seeing Jesus in the Scriptures

In John 5:19, Jesus stated that 'the Son can do nothing by himself; he can do only what he sees his Father doing'. On the face of it, this seems ridiculous. This is Jesus we're talking about! He walked on water and cast out demons, He battled with Satan and threw the money changers from the temple courts, He publicly mocked the Jewish leaders and did countless other amazing things… and yet He couldn't do anything without looking to His Father! Jesus demonstrates for us the greatest humility of all – He is God, and yet He willingly put Himself in a position of absolute reliance on His Father.

WEEK TWO

# Caleb gets his inheritance

## Opening Icebreaker

Have you ever been consumed by a hobby? (I recently took up the violin and was so committed I had countless lessons, bought a vintage instrument and bow, and spent hours watching YouTube videos!) Why don't you share your experiences and see if anyone has been similarly consumed by some activity or pastime?

## Bible Readings

- Joshua 13–15 (if short of time, read 14:6–15; 15:13–19)
- Numbers 14:20–24
- 1 Kings 11:6
- 1 Corinthians 15:58
- Ephesians 6:7–8

**Key verse:** Joshua 14:9

**Focus:** Serving God means following Him wholeheartedly.

## Opening Our Eyes

Do you recall the famous story about Shammua and Palti?
Or the accounts of Gaddiel and Nahbi? It is no surprise if you
don't, because they were some of the nay-saying spies who
joined Joshua when Moses sent him to check out the Promised
Land. Caleb, however, you *will* remember, because he was
the one who came back from that mission with the faith-filled
report that 'We should go up and take possession of the land,
for we can certainly do it' (Num. 13:30). Unfortunately, those
other spies – the forgettable ones – outvoted him and, as a
result, God made the Israelites wander in the wilderness for
40 years until that whole generation had died out. Except, of
course, for Joshua and Caleb.

In Numbers 14, God mentions Caleb by name to Moses,
saying, 'because my servant Caleb has a different spirit and
follows me wholeheartedly, I will bring him into the land
he went to, and his descendants will inherit it' (v24). The
word 'wholeheartedly' in this verse is elsewhere translated
'completely' or 'fully', and apart from David in 1 Kings 11:6,
Caleb is the only person in the Old Testament described in
this way. Caleb followed the Lord completely, with everything
that was in him, and so his service to God did not end with
spying out the land.

It is now 45 years later, and Caleb is 85 – the kind of age
when you might expect him to be retiring and looking back
rather than fighting and looking ahead. Yet you can sense his
eagerness and passion in his statement to Joshua: 'I am still as
strong today as the day Moses sent me out; I'm just as vigorous
to go out to battle now as I was then' (Josh. 14:11).

Somewhat ironically, Joshua gives him land that is occupied
by the Anakites, who were giants – the very thing that
undermined the faith of their fellow spies all those years

before. We see in chapter 15 that 'From Hebron Caleb drove out the three Anakites' (v14) and it's not hard to imagine him rooting them out single-handedly!

Caleb then challenges the faith of his tribesmen, offering his own daughter to the man who takes the city of Kiriath Sepher, and his nephew Othniel rises to the challenge. This is the first mention of Othniel, but we meet him again in the book of Judges, where he is the first and arguably the greatest of the judges, acting in unison with God as he brings judgment on Cushan-Rishathaim: 'the LORD... raised up for them a deliverer, Othniel son of Kenaz, Caleb's younger brother, who saved them' (Judg. 3:9). Clearly a man of faith and action, inspired no doubt by Caleb.

Finally, we see Caleb's daughter asking her father for springs of water to go with the land he had given her, and Caleb gives her not just one of the springs but both 'the upper and lower springs' (Josh. 15:19) – double what she asked for.

And so, in these two brief stories about Caleb, we see in him what it means to follow God wholeheartedly – to the full. First, he doesn't only look back to past testimonies, but forges new ones in his service to the Lord. Second, he inspires faithful service in others, challenging them and presenting himself a role model. And third, he demonstrates godliness in his treatment of others.

## Discussion Starters

1.  What, if anything, surprised you as you read through these two accounts of Caleb's latter years?

    _____
    _____
    _____
    _____
    _____

2.  Read 1 Corinthians 15:58 and Ephesians 6:7–8. In both passages, Paul speaks of wholehearted (full) service. How might such service be both desirable and possible?

    _____
    _____
    _____
    _____
    _____

3.  In what way is our relationship with the Holy Spirit vital for such service?

    _____
    _____
    _____
    _____
    _____

4.  In Numbers 14:20–24, God spoke of Caleb's 'different spirit'. What do you understand by this phrase, and how might we cultivate a different spirit in ourselves?

    _____
    _____
    _____
    _____
    _____

**5.** Have there been people in your life who have inspired your faith and encouraged you in your service to God?

_____

_____

_____

_____

_____

**6.** Share a recent testimony of God's work in your life.

_____

_____

_____

_____

_____

**7.** If a new Christian asked you to explain the role of the Holy Spirit in a believer's life, what would you say?

_____

_____

_____

_____

_____

## Personal Application

With over seven and a half billion people in the world at the time of writing this book, it can be hard to see how our individual lives might have any real significance. Hard to see, that is, until you consider that God – the one who made the universe and everything in it, and who holds it all together – has given us the opportunity to serve Him. Just consider the enormity of that for a moment.

We were created to serve God, to further His reign and rule in the world, to spread His message of good news for all humanity, and to promote godliness, justice, grace and mercy. There is no greater task! And while the world might consider the rich and the famous, the successful and beautiful, and the important people of history to be of most significance, there is nothing we can do of more worth than serving the Lord.

## Seeing Jesus in the Scriptures

Here's a question for you: in His service to God, do you think Jesus ever did anything that was insignificant? In the previous session, we saw that Jesus looked to His Father for everything He did – doing nothing without His guidance. As a result of this moment-by-moment interaction with the Holy Spirit, Jesus lived the most significant life that has ever been lived.

Take some time to think of examples of His wholehearted service as recorded in the Gospels, whether it be from His childhood desire to be in His Father's house, His interaction with His followers, the miracles He performed or His journey to the cross.

WEEK THREE

# Taking the Promised Land

## Opening Icebreaker

As a child, I hated cleaning my teeth and avoided it whenever possible. Now, many fillings and angry dentists later, I believe that cleaning my teeth is good for me, so I brush and floss every day (sometimes twice!). Share examples of beliefs that are demonstrated by the way you live.

## Bible Readings

- Joshua 16–19 (if short of time read 17:7–18:10)
- Genesis 12:7
- Joshua 21:44–45
- James 2:18–24
- Hebrews 11:1,6
- Romans 14:23

**Key verse:** Joshua 18:3

**Focus:** We serve God when our actions are shaped by our faith.

## Opening Our Eyes

The chapters detailing Israel's tribal allotments are not generally considered the most thrilling. It's quite a change from the action of earlier chapters. While we may love reading about how the walls of Jericho came tumbling down, and when God made the sun stand still for an extra day, we aren't so keen on the 29 southernmost towns of the tribe of Judah in the Negev toward the boundary of Edom. But while the long stream of hard-to-pronounce names may not be especially riveting to us today, what is happening here is of huge importance.

Back in Genesis, God called Abram to leave his people and travel to this same land, telling him, 'To your offspring I will give this land' (Gen. 12:7). That was around 450 years ago. So much has happened since then: the birth (and near-sacrifice) of Isaac, Jacob and his 12 sons, Joseph and the years of slavery in Egypt, Moses and the years of wandering in the wilderness. Throughout that time, the people clung to the promise that they would be given this land, despite it seeming impossible. And now, here they are! They are not only *in* the land, but it is *their* land.

Almost.

As we read through the lists of the allotments, a few problems emerge (see Josh. 15:63; 16:10; 17:12). And it isn't just these three tribes. In the opening chapter of the book of Judges, we read a similar list of failures involving Benjamin, Zebulun, Asher, Naphtali and Dan (vv21–34). Consider this in the light of the closing statements of the tribal allotments in Joshua 21: 'The LORD gave them rest on every side, just as he had sworn to their ancestors. Not one of their enemies withstood them; the LORD gave all their enemies into their hands. Not one of all the LORD's good promises to Israel failed; every one was fulfilled' (vv44–45).

On the one hand, God promised that the Israelites would drive out the Canaanites, yet on the other we see most of the tribes failing to do so. Old Testament history shows they never drove them out! What is going on here?

The problem is certainly not on God's side. As He declared through Balaam in Numbers 23:19: 'God is not human, that he should lie... Does he promise and not fulfil?' No. God fulfils His promises. The problem is with the Israelites. Throughout the Bible there is a connection drawn between God's word and people's work. In the book of Joshua alone, God has told Joshua that He would part the Jordan, that He would bring down the walls of Jericho, that He would give the southern and northern kings into his hands. In response, Joshua had to send the ark into the Jordan, he had to march around Jericho for seven days, and he had to engage the enemy coalitions in battle. Had Joshua not responded to God's word with these faithful actions, it is doubtful whether those things would have come to pass.

When we read of the Israelites repeatedly failing to drive out the Canaanites, what we see is that their faith has failed them; faced with a powerful enemy, they don't believe God will give them the victory. So when Joshua questions the Israelites, saying, 'How long will you wait before you begin to take possession of the land that the LORD... has given you?" (Josh. 18:3), you can sense his frustration with them. They've seen God's promise to drive out the people fulfilled over and over again, but their faith is weak, and their failure to respond to God's word will eventually be their undoing.

## Discussion Starters

1.  Share anything from these four chapters that surprised you or raised questions for you.

    _____

    _____

    _____

    _____

2.  Why do you think the Israelites failed to drive out the inhabitants of the land in spite of God's promise that they would?

    _____

    _____

    _____

    _____

3.  Read James 2:18–24. This is a somewhat controversial passage, seeming to conflict with the Bible's clear teaching that our salvation is through faith alone, not by our works. What do you understand to be the relationship between faith and works?

    _____

    _____

    _____

    _____

4.  In Hebrews 11:1, the writer defines faith as 'confidence in what we hope for and assurance about what we do not see'. How would you define faith?

    _____

    _____

    _____

    _____

**5.** Consider some of the great promises in Scripture
(John 3:16; Rom. 8:28; 1 Cor. 10:13; Phil. 4:19; 1 John 1:9).
In what way might your faith in these promises shape the
way you live your life?

_____

_____

_____

_____

**6.** How might it be possible to fail to enter into God's
promises, whether those in Scripture or personal
promises we have received?

_____

_____

_____

_____

**7.** In addition to biblical promises and guidance, we are
called to 'live by the Spirit' (Gal. 5:16) – to act according
to His guidance. If a new believer asked you to explain
how to hear and recognise the Holy Spirit's voice, what
would you say?

_____

_____

_____

_____

## Personal Application

In Hebrews 11:6, the writer tells us that 'without faith it is impossible to please God' and Paul goes even further to say that 'everything that does not come from faith is sin' (Rom. 14:23). Just think about that for a moment. Everything – all we have ever done and ever will do – that is not done in faith is considered sinful!

This seems extreme, and somewhat disheartening. But actually, it makes sense. If faith is believing that what God has said is true, then acting in faith is simply living out this belief. And we have seen that the Holy Spirit is with us to constantly teach us and remind us that at every moment we can choose to act in faith and 'walk by the Spirit' or to act in accordance with our own wills.

## Seeing Jesus in the Scriptures

Scholars claim that there are around a hundred prophecies in the Old Testament that were fulfilled in the life of Jesus – from His birth as a human in Bethlehem through to His death on the cross. So why did God decide to sow the Old Testament with so many prophecies and promises about His Son? Well, not only do these give us all the proof we need that Jesus really is God, but they build our faith in the associated promises of forgiveness and grace, of mercy and salvation, of eternal life and love. Let's rejoice together in the certainty that 'no matter how many promises God has made, they are "Yes" in Christ' (2 Cor. 1:20).

WEEK FOUR

# The gift of special cities

## Opening Icebreaker

Come up with as many examples as you can of how something good being scattered or spread around is better than it all being in one place (eg spreading yeast through dough for an even rise, and scattering poppy seeds over a meadow for a more idyllic view).

## Bible Readings

- Joshua 20–21 (if short of time read 20:1–21:5)
- Genesis 49:7
- Deuteronomy 18:1–2
- Matthew 6:25–33
- Acts 20:35
- Matthew 5:13–16

**Key verse:** Joshua 21:41

**Focus:** Our service to God will have an effect on those around us.

## Opening Our Eyes

Having cast lots and divided the land between eleven of
the tribes (Ephraim and the two halves of Manasseh being
counted as the one tribe of Joseph), Joshua's attention turns
to the Levites. They were something of a special case. Back in
Genesis 49, Jacob gathered his sons together and pronounced
blessings over them, although some of them are more like
curses. For example, to Levi and Simeon he said, 'Cursed be
their anger, so fierce, and their fury, so cruel! I will scatter
them in Jacob and disperse them in Israel' (v7). The land
allotted to Simeon was tucked away inside that given to Judah.
The Levites, however, had no land. But that didn't mean they
were left with nothing.

When Moses was up on Mount Sinai receiving the tablets
of the law and Aaron built a golden calf for the Israelites to
worship, only the Levites kept themselves separate, refusing
to join in the idolatry. As a result, they were chosen to be
the tribe to carry the ark and serve in the tabernacle. In
Deuteronomy 18, Moses states: 'The Levitical priests – indeed,
the whole tribe of Levi – are to have no land allotted to them
or any inheritance with Israel. They shall live on the food
offerings presented to the LORD, for that is their inheritance.
They shall have no inheritance among their fellow Israelites;
the LORD is their inheritance' (vv1–2).

If you read through the list of the cities the Levites settled
in, you'll note that each of the other tribes had to give them
cities from their own inheritance – 48 in all. It would be easy
to imagine the other tribes not being delighted at this, and
yet there is no mention of reluctance – they hand their cities
over willingly, allowing the Levites to spread themselves
throughout, salted across the land.

At this time, the tabernacle has been set up in Shiloh, a handily central location where it will remain for around three hundred years until the time of David. This is the place where the Levitical priests will perform the various sacrifices and offerings required in the law. But not all of them. Most of them will live in the 48 cities they've been given, where they are to 'teach the Israelites all the decrees the LORD has given them through Moses' (Lev. 10:11). This role includes ensuring everyone knows about God and about the law, and also making sure it is upheld, being called upon to judge transgressions and disputes as necessary. This is why the 'cities of refuge', detailed in Joshua 20, are all cities inhabited by Levites. These cities are as spread out as the Levites themselves, with no city more than 30 miles from the next, so the accidental murderers fleeing to them can get there within a single day's journey. The role of the Levites isn't just to dish out punishments, but also to make sure people are treated fairly, and to offer refuge to those who deserve it.

As such, the Levites offer a great service to the other Israelites. Yes, they've cost them a few cities, but in return they will receive vital teaching that will help them and their descendants to keep themselves holy, they will receive fair judgment, and they will have the vast amount of sacrifices and other rituals taken care of that allow them to survive with God living in their midst. Not a bad exchange for a few settlements that weren't even theirs to begin with!

## Discussion Starters

1. What struck you most in this account of the Levitical cities and 'cities of refuge'?

2. The Levites had no way of providing for themselves – instead they relied on the tithes and generosity of the other tribes, while they dedicated themselves to serving God. How does this relate to Jesus' call to us to seek God's kingdom above all else (see Matt. 6:25–33)?

3. In Acts 20:35, Paul quotes Jesus: 'It is more blessed to give than to receive.' In what way did the Israelite tribes receive blessing through giving cities to the Levites?

4. Give examples from your life or the lives of others that demonstrate that giving is more blessed than receiving.

**5.** Why do you think God wanted to spread the Levites throughout the other tribes? What might have been the result of giving them their own allotment instead?

_____

_____

_____

_____

**6.** Read Matthew 5:13–16. What do you understand by the terms 'salt of the earth' and 'light of the world', and in what way do they relate to Jesus' followers?

_____

_____

_____

_____

**7.** How can we be salt and light in our Christian communities, inspiring others by our wholehearted following of Jesus, without coming across as holier-than-thou?

_____

_____

_____

_____

## Personal Application

In Matthew 5, after calling His followers 'the light of the world' (v14), Jesus goes on to talk about towns on hills and lamps under bowls. His point being that lights are meant to shine, and that we, His followers, can't hide ourselves from the world in which we live. Unless you're a hermit hiding in a forgotten cave, you mix with other people, both believers and non-believers. You are seen by them and your life has an impact on them, no matter how small. Like the Levites, we have been salted throughout the world to be God's light, demonstrating godliness, speaking truth and acting in love. There are dangers when it comes to mixing with others, as we'll see in Week Six, but take the time to consider today: who sees you?

## Seeing Jesus in the Scriptures

The 'cities of refuge' are often referred to as a 'type of Christ' – a phrase meaning they teach us something about Jesus. Joshua, for example, is a type of Christ, because he saved God's people, bringing them from the wilderness into their promised inheritance, much like Jesus saves us, bringing us from death into our future inheritance as God's people. In Hebrews 6, the writer talks of our hope in God's promise saying, 'we who have fled to take hold of the hope set before us may be greatly encouraged' (v18). The Greek verb used here means to flee to a place of refuge, in this case referring to Jesus, our 'high priest for ever' (v20). In Him, we find eternal refuge from the death that was the penalty for our sin.

WEEK FIVE

# Conflict across the Jordan

## Opening Icebreaker

As a group, have a go at solving a selection of Rebus puzzles (also known as Dingbats) together.

## Bible Readings

- Joshua 22
- Joshua 1:12–18
- James 3:3–8
- 1 Corinthians 12:12–27
- John 17:20–23

**Key verse:** Joshua 22:11–12

**Focus:** Our unity as God's people is vital if we are to serve Him effectively.

## Opening Our Eyes

As the Israelites start spreading throughout the land to take their inheritance, the natural division of the Jordan river threatens to tear them apart. Moses gave to the tribes of Reuben and Gad, together with half the tribe of Manasseh, land east of the river; land in which they had settled many years before. When God called the people to enter Canaan, the men of the two and a half tribes left their homes and families to help with the campaign, promising Joshua, 'Whatever you have commanded us we will do, and wherever you send us we will go' (Josh. 1:16).

Now that the campaign is over, Joshua blesses them, saying 'You have done all that Moses the servant of the LORD commanded, and you have obeyed me in everything I commanded' (Josh. 22:2), and calling them 'to love the LORD your God, to walk in obedience to him, to keep his commands, to hold fast to him and to serve him with all your heart and with all your soul' (Josh. 22:5). But as they head home, they pause on the western bank of the Jordan to build a large altar. And then the trouble begins.

You can almost imagine the gossip that takes place once the other Israelites come across this altar. James tells us that 'the tongue... is a fire' (James 3:6). Gratitude for their help in the campaign disappears as soon as the Israelites hear about the two and half tribes building an altar on *their* land. Very quickly, the sparks fly, the fires of anger, discord and violence are ignited, and the Israelites gather and decide to attack them.

It's telling to note the lack of Joshua's input in the rest of this chapter; he's been excluded from this war meeting. Instead they draft in Phinehas, the high priest's son. He appears back in Numbers 25, where a plague was killing off the Israelites because they were intermarrying with the Moabites. Phinehas witnessed one of these couples heading into a tent, so he followed and drove a spear into them, which ended the plague. He's known as a man who tackles Israelite misbehaviour with swift and deadly force, so a perfect choice for this situation.

The Canaan-dwelling Israelites talk themselves into believing that the two and a half tribes have set up the altar as an alternative to the tabernacle, a rebellion against God. Not that they are that concerned about God's feelings; rather what God might do to them, as we see when Phinehas confronts them: 'If you rebel against the Lord today, tomorrow he will be angry with the whole community of Israel' (Josh. 22:18). Note that Phinehas doesn't simply ask them why they built the altar – his mind is already made up.

The tribes from east of the Jordan might easily have responded with anger to such an accusation, which would surely have led to civil war. But they don't. Instead they reply with grace and clear explanation, calling on the Lord Himself to bear witness, stating they built the altar '"not for burnt offerings or sacrifices." On the contrary, it is to be a witness between us and you and the generations that follow, that we will worship the LORD' (Josh. 22:26–27). They're concerned that the barrier of the Jordan will make them seem like second-class citizens, less important than their fellow tribes. They built the altar as a reminder for them all that they are united, together, as the people of God.

Thankfully, Phinehas accepts their explanation, bringing joy to the whole community. As Proverbs 15:1 says, 'A gentle answer turns away wrath'. And so, the land is settled, the people are united.

## Discussion Starters

1. Share any surprises or questions that arose as you went through this passage.

   _____

   _____

   _____

   _____

   _____

2. Why do you think the Israelites in Canaan chose Phinehas to represent them against the two and a half tribes from east of the Jordan instead of consulting Joshua?

   _____

   _____

   _____

   _____

   _____

3. Read James 3:3–8. Share experiences of when people's tongues have been a force for good or for evil.

   _____

   _____

   _____

   _____

   _____

4. 'Without wood a fire goes out; without a gossip a quarrel dies down' (Prov. 26:20). Why do you think gossip, slander and the like are condemned throughout Scripture?

   _____

   _____

   _____

   _____

   _____

**5.** Consider the following verses (Psa. 133:1; John 13:34; Eph. 4:3; Phil. 2:2; 1 Pet. 3:8). Why is our unity so important to God, and what is the connection between love and unity?

_____

_____

_____

_____

**6.** The tribes that settled in the Promised Land considered themselves more important than the two and a half that lived on the other side of the Jordan. How might humility help in our battle for unity, and how can we cultivate humility in our lives?

_____

_____

_____

_____

**7.** If someone asked you why there is disunity in the Church – as demonstrated by the many denominations and disagreements over doctrine – what would you say?

_____

_____

_____

_____

## Personal Application

In recent years, Christianity has become an increasingly 'personal' matter – the focus being placed on *my* relationship with God, instead of *our* relationship with God. This wasn't always the case. When we look at the Early Church, the emphasis is on community and coming together as God's people. The New Testament images of the Church as a body, a temple and a family all point to this fact. This doesn't mean each individual is not important and distinct, but our unity must be a priority. As Paul says in 1 Corinthians 12, 'there should be no division in the body... its parts should have equal concern for each other. If one part suffers, every part suffers with it; if one part is honoured, every part rejoices with it' (vv25–26). Why not take some time to pray for your church community?

## Seeing Jesus in the Scriptures

On the night He was betrayed, Jesus prayed for all His followers – which includes us – saying, 'I pray also for those who will believe in me through (my disciples') message, that all of them may be one, Father, just as you are in me and I am in you... I in them and you in me – so that they may be brought to complete unity. Then the world will know that you sent me and have loved them even as you have loved me' (John 17:20–21,23). Did you notice that last sentence? Take a little time to meditate on the enormity of what Jesus is saying. Our unity is proof that the gospel is true!

WEEK SIX

# The Canaanite problem

## Opening Icebreaker

Play a word association game. One person chooses a word to begin (eg car), then the next says a word associated with it (train), then the next (teach) and so on. Players are eliminated if they take too long, repeat words or the group disagrees that there's a connection. The last player left wins.

## Bible Readings

- Joshua 23
- Deuteronomy 7:2
- Judges 3:7
- Matthew 6:24
- John 14:23–24

**Key verse:** Joshua 23:7

**Focus:** Our service to God requires devotion to Him above all else.

## Opening Our Eyes

Back in Week Three, we saw that most of the Israelite tribes failed to overpower the Canaanites living in their allotted land – a demonstration of their lack of faith in God's promise to drive them out. Now, several years later, Joshua reminds them of that promise: 'The LORD your God himself will push them out for your sake' (Josh. 23:5). The rest of this speech is focused on the issue of getting rid of this indigenous folk, harking back to God's command to 'destroy them totally. Make no treaty with them, and show them no mercy' (Deut. 7:2). This is not an optional extra to the Israelites possessing the land; if they are going to be God's people, they must remove the Canaanites – not just most of them, but *all*.

In the first session, we raised the question: 'Why is God so ungracious towards the Canaanites?' Isn't He a forgiving and merciful God? These are valid questions. Important questions. Questions that need answering if we're to avoid the mistake of picturing the 'Old Testament God' as an angry, vengeful judge, compared with the nice, don't-worry-about-sin 'New Testament God'. Both views are, of course, inaccurate – God does judge sin, but He always acts in love and for the good of His people.

Four and a half centuries earlier, when Abram visited Canaan, it was full of people worshipping false gods. These idols demanded forms of worship that were despicable to God: 'they do all kinds of detestable things the LORD hates. They even burn their sons and daughters in the fire as sacrifices to their gods' (Deut. 12:31). Instead of wiping them out there and then, however, God gave the Canaanites time to see the error of their ways – over four hundred years to repent and worship Him.

They didn't.

And so God issues the order to wipe them out, hardening their hearts and vowing to give them into the hands of the Israelites. But – and this is important – He did not command this out of hatred for the Canaanites, but out of love for His people. God has set apart the Israelites to serve Him, which we've seen is the most significant and worthwhile way to live, and to allow them to live together with the Canaanites would undermine this.

In the previous session, we saw how, for a time, the Israelites intermarried with the Moabites, 'who invited them to the sacrifices to their gods. The people ate the sacrificial meal and bowed down before these gods' (Num. 25:2). In a single verse, they went from mixing with the Moabites to worshipping their gods! Mixing with the Canaanites was just as dangerous.

Joshua reminds the Israelites of the necessity of getting rid of the inhabitants of the land, because it's vital for their own protection to do so: 'they will become snares and traps for you, whips on your backs and thorns in your eyes' (Josh. 23:13). And so he calls on the people to demonstrate their love for God by obeying His command to drive out the Canaanites.

Sadly, they fail to do so and, as the Old Testament unfolds, we see the results of them mixing with the Canaanites: 'The Israelites did evil in the eyes of the LORD; they forgot the LORD their God and served the Baals and the Asherahs' (Judg. 3:7). In the end, it was for this reason that Assyria scattered the northern kingdom of Israel and then Babylon took the kingdom of Judah into exile.

## Discussion Starters

1. Joshua correctly predicted the Israelites would be drawn into idolatry by mixing with the Canaanites. Why do you think this was the case?

_____

_____

_____

_____

2. Read Jesus' words in Matthew 6:24. What other idols are worshipped in your society? Why is it still so easy to be seduced by such idols?

_____

_____

_____

_____

3. The following verses discourage us from bad influences (Psa. 1:1; Prov. 13:20; Rom. 16:17; 1 Cor. 15:33). How is it possible to maintain a balance between being in the world and being set apart?

_____

_____

_____

_____

4. Peter talks about some people's response to followers of Jesus: 'They are surprised that you do not join them in their reckless, wild living, and they heap abuse on you' (1 Pet. 4:4). Share experiences where similar 'surprise' has resulted in either positive or negative responses.

_____

_____

_____

_____

**5.** In his speech, Joshua draws a link between obedience and love (Josh. 23:6,11). Read John 14:23–24, in which Jesus makes a similar connection. Why do they go together, do you think?

_____

_____

_____

_____

**6.** How do you find love and obedience work together in your own experience?

_____

_____

_____

_____

**7.** The command to love God is often repeated in Scripture. Is it possible to love by command? And if so, how does this work in practice?

_____

_____

_____

_____

## Personal Application

This is the third week where we've considered our relationship with other people, and this time it comes with a warning. In our mixing with others, we are to be wary of the effect they may have on us.

At the same time, we are called to be a good influence on others, both in and outside the Church. As Proverbs 27:17 says, 'As iron sharpens iron, so one person sharpens another', and Paul encouraged Timothy (and us) to 'set an example for the believers in speech, in conduct, in love, in faith and in purity' (1 Tim. 4:12).

Reflect for a moment on your interaction with others, and the influence you may be having on one another.

## Seeing Jesus in the Scriptures

We have been reminded in these sessions of the constant, intimate connection between Jesus and His Father. The reality of Jesus' great love for God is clear, and it is shown throughout His life. Not only did Jesus obey His Father's guidance in all He did and said – He demonstrated absolute obedience to the ultimate degree.

It is best summed up in Paul's words in Philippians 2, where he calls us to 'have the same mindset as Christ Jesus: who, being in very nature God, did not consider equality with God something to be used to his own advantage; rather, he made himself nothing by taking the very nature of a servant, being made in human likeness. And being found in appearance as a man, he humbled himself by becoming obedient to death – even death on a cross!' (vv5–8).

WEEK SEVEN

# The Israelites make a choice

## Opening Icebreaker

My most recent New Year's resolution was to go for a long walk every day, I even bought special shoes for it. On 2 January I walked for about 40 minutes and found it quite tiring – I haven't done it since! Share resolutions (New Year's or otherwise) you have made and how long, or short, they lasted.

## Bible Readings

- Joshua 24
- Genesis 35:4
- Romans 12:1–2
- Psalm 100:1–2
- Hebrews 12:1–2

**Key verse:** Joshua 24:15

**Focus:** Choosing to serve God is not easy, but it is the best choice we can make… every day.

## Opening Our Eyes

What a journey the Israelites have had, from wanderers to warriors, from strays to settlers. They crossed the Jordan, they destroyed Jericho and Aii, they defeated the southern kings and the northern coalition, they then divided up the land and took their allotments, bringing to pass what had been promised to Abraham.

Or so they might have assumed. Joshua makes it clear who was really behind their success. He delivers a message from God, detailing events from the calling of Abram, through the bondage in Egypt and the raising up of Moses, to the taking of the land itself. In the NIV, the word 'I' occurs 18 times in verses 3–13, though in the Hebrew, God is actually the subject of 23 of the verbs.

The message is clear: God is the real force behind all that has happened to the Israelites. Without Him, they would not have defeated the Canaanites, they would have had no sustenance in the wilderness, they would not have escaped from Egypt, in fact, they would have never existed in the first place. The Israelites may have thought they got to where they were through their own might and merit, but they didn't even build the houses they live in or plant the crops that sustain them. This isn't to detract from the necessity of their faithful actions – as we saw in Week Three – but those actions only succeeded because God allowed it.

'Now' says Joshua, having humbled the people and opened their eyes to the truth, 'fear the LORD and serve him with all faithfulness' (Josh. 24:14). It may seem crazy to have to make this statement to the Israelites, the nation who were known as 'God's people', but serving God isn't the easy option!

As we've seen in these few weeks, serving God means relying on Him alone, responding to His guidance with faithful actions. It involves wholehearted commitment to Him, living in unity with all God's people, and being a light to the world, while keeping ourselves from ungodly influences. It would be far easier to serve a made-up god instead – a god like Baal, made out of wood or stone – a god that didn't want a relationship. And yet that would mean serving a god that was not real.

Joshua knows all this and understands that he's presenting them with a difficult choice: 'But if serving the LORD seems undesirable to you, then choose for yourselves this day whom you will serve' (Josh. 24:15). The people's response is enthusiastic. Of course they choose to serve God! After all He's done for them, it's the obvious choice. And yet you sense Joshua's sorrow in his reply: 'You are not able to serve the LORD. He is a holy God; he is a jealous God. He will not forgive your rebellion and your sins' (Josh. 24:19). The people, however, are adamant, believing themselves perfectly capable of serving Him, so he calls them to get rid of their idols right in the very place Jacob buried his idols in Genesis 35.

So the Israelites renew the covenant, promising with great passion that they will serve God. And there we leave them, returning to their allotted lands, full of zeal and eagerness... but you need only turn the page of your Bible to see how long their vow lasted. Joshua is buried there by the tabernacle, his life of faithful service finally at an end, but the story of the Israelites continues – the time of the judges has come.

## Discussion Starters

**1.** What struck you in this closing chapter of the book of Joshua?

_____

_____

_____

_____

**2.** Joshua opened the eyes of the Israelites to the fact that God was the force behind everything that had happened to them. Consider the following verses, which emphasise this (Psa. 135:6; Prov. 16:33; Rom. 8:28; Eph. 3:20). What difference might it make to have our eyes open to God's work in all things?

_____

_____

_____

_____

**3.** Read Romans 12:1. Some more literal Bible translations change 'worship' to 'service'. How would you define the word 'worship', and what is the relationship between worship and service?

_____

_____

_____

_____

**4.** Psalm 100:2 says: 'Worship [or serve] the LORD with gladness'. We are called to serve God even when it hurts. How might such service bring gladness and joy?

_____

_____

_____

_____

**5.** In the previous session, we looked at how idolatry is still just as much a problem today as it was in Joshua's time. In what way might idol worship ultimately be considered self-worship?

_____

_____

_____

_____

**6.** What difficulties may stand in the way of our service to God? In what ways might we be better equipped to serve the Lord than the Israelites?

_____

_____

_____

_____

**7.** If a new believer asked you how to serve God, what would you say?

_____

_____

_____

_____

## Personal Application

We have a choice. Will we serve God or will we serve ourselves? Take the time to consider all we have seen in this book about what it means to serve God. Ultimately it involves a relationship. A relationship in which we look to God for His constant guidance and respond with faithful action (or sometimes faithful *inaction*), regardless of how we might feel.

Serving God is not easy, but it is the best, most fulfilling and most joyful way to live. And it's not a choice we make once, but a decision that is presented to us fresh each morning: 'choose for yourselves this day whom you will serve' (Josh. 24:15).

## Seeing Jesus in the Scriptures

As we saw in the previous session, Jesus demonstrated absolute obedience, serving God even to death. It can be easy to think of service and obedience as drudgery, like a slave serving a demanding master or a child obeying an overbearing parent. But consider the words from Hebrews 12:1–2. Did you notice that little word in there, the thing that motivated Jesus? Joy!

Not that He enjoyed the battles with Satan and the Jewish authorities, the rejection by His family, His friends and fellow Jews, the difficulties of living in this world, the humiliation, whipping and the most painful death imaginable... But in the midst of it, He had the joy of knowing that He was serving His Father, and that through His life and death, He opened a way for us to be God's children and have eternity with Him to look forward to.

# Leader's Notes

These notes are designed to help you lead the weekly studies in a group. Please take the time to read through the notes beforehand to help with your preparation. It is also worth reading through the 'Personal Application' and 'Seeing Jesus in the Scriptures' sections to get a feel for the direction of each session.

The overarching theme of the second half of the book of Joshua is serving God, looking to Him for constant guidance and meeting it with faithful action.

## Week One: The campaign's conclusion

In this opening session, the focus is on reliance on God.

### Opening Icebreaker

Each session's icebreaker is both a team-building exercise and an object lesson, linking to an aspect of the study. In this case, the idea is pride – believing we can do something on our own without the help of God or others. Hopefully the person who is taking on the entire rest of the group won't actually beat them!

If no one volunteers to be the lone player, pick someone yourself. You'll need to get the paper ready in advance, whether it be old newspaper or other waste paper ready for recycling. You'll also need a couple of similar sized receptacles for them to aim at.

## Bible Readings

All the sessions in this book have a number of verses from
other parts of the Bible. It is not necessary to read these
together at the beginning, as they are mainly used in the
discussion starters, but it would certainly be beneficial to
read the main passage together, which is always the top
one. Where studies cover more than one chapter of Joshua,
I have suggested key passages that you could read together.
It is still worth asking the group to read the whole section
before you meet.

## Key Verse

In this verse, we see God not only encouraging Joshua with
the certainty of victory against the massive forces of Jabin,
but also instructing him to hamstring the horses and burn
the chariots – a command that is all about trusting God
instead of worldly strength (see 'Opening Our Eyes' section).

## Discussion Starters

1.  This open question, encouraging people to share what
    was most striking for them from the passage, will be
    the starter for each week. The aim here is to help people
    to start talking, so it is worth trying to avoid getting too
    bogged down with details, debates or depths.

2.  'Pride' tends to have two senses in modern English. First,
    it is used to describe a feeling of satisfaction or pleasure
    in either one's own achievements or those of someone
    else. The second, and the one we're focusing on here, is
    the belief that you do not need the help of God or others,
    but that you can get along just fine in your own strength.

3-4. The focus here is not necessarily on plumbing the
    depths of each person's most sinful desires, but on
    turning them into strengths – hopefully coming to
    the conclusion that we need to ask God for help and

guidance, throwing ourselves on His grace. (It may be worth considering the promise of 1 Cor. 10:13.)

**5.** This is really two questions: identifying the strengths, then considering ways of relying on God instead of these strengths. For example, I tend to see myself as being good at writing – so I spend a lot of time reading books by people whose writing is leagues better than mine, which is both humbling and helps me to rely more on God's guidance when I write. Perhaps share an example from your own life to get the ball rolling.

**6.** This question tends to provoke some robust discussion, with some being adamant that we should run every decision (down to what clothes to wear or what to have for lunch) past God, while others considering the suggestion to be utterly impractical. It may be worth reading the 'Seeing Jesus in the Scriptures' section together and considering whether Jesus ran every decision past His Father, and how this might have worked practically for Him.

**7.** This is potentially a good opportunity to think deeper about church life, but try to steer the discussion away from anything that could promote gossip and divisive talk. It may be a good opportunity to pray together for your church community.

## **Week Two:** Caleb gets his inheritance

This week looks at the two short accounts of how Caleb demonstrates wholehearted service to God, what such service looks like, and why it is desirable for us today.

### Opening Icebreaker

This icebreaker is all about becoming consumed with
hobbies, pastimes and such like – the point being that this
gives us an insight into wholehearted service and how it is
possible. As this is a 'sharing' icebreaker, it is worth coming
up with an example or two from your own life to get the
conversation started.

### Bible Readings

The two sections listed in the brackets are the ones this
week's study focuses on. For the sake of completeness, it is
worth asking the group to read through the rest of the three
chapters in their own time.

### Key Verse

This is the verse that uses the word 'wholeheartedly' and is
spoken by the 85-year-old Caleb as a prelude to driving out a
settlement of giants!

### Discussion Starters

2.   Both verses talk about serving God wholeheartedly/
     fully, with the first stating that our service to God is not
     in vain, and the second giving the promise of reward for
     such service. It may be worth raising these as points to
     discuss, especially the idea of being rewarded by God,
     which is perhaps not a topic often raised by Christians.
     As for the possibility of wholehearted service, don't
     forget the illustration of the icebreaker.

3.   This discussion starter is linked to number 7, so don't
     get too bogged down in detail, as this can be examined
     in greater depth through role-playing. It is worth
     reminding the group about the 'Seeing Jesus in the
     Scriptures' section from the first week, in which we saw
     Him taking constant guidance from the Holy Spirit.

**4.**　My own thought, for what it's worth, is that, while the other spies were adamant the Israelites could not take the Promised Land, Caleb wasn't afraid to contradict them. Sometimes, the world needs people who will stand up and say there is a different way – a better way – to think and act.

**5-6.**　As these two discussion starters are about sharing personal experiences, it is worth thinking of some examples from your own life beforehand so you can get the ball rolling if needed. The reason for coming up with a *recent* testimony of God's work in your life is that wholehearted service results in constant interaction with the Holy Spirit and therefore daily testimonies. That said, it's important to make it clear that testimonies don't always have to be 'big' things – they can be as simple as feeling God prompt you to do the washing up instead of leaving it for someone else to do.

**7.**　It may be worth tackling this question as a role-playing exercise, with the group splitting into pairs so they can take turns playing the part of the Christian and the new Christian. While it may appear the role of the new Christian is only a small one, as an interested listener, they need to encourage the speaker to give more information and ask pertinent questions. The Christian, on the other hand, will need to avoid the use of jargon, assuming their audience has little prior knowledge of Christianity.

## **Week Three:** Taking the Promised Land

Rather than focusing on the land distribution itself, this session tackles the issue of the towns and areas the Israelites failed to take due to their lack of faith in God's promise.

As such, this week's study looks at the relationship between God's word and our faithful response.

### Opening Icebreaker

The aim of this icebreaker is to demonstrate that our actions (together with our thoughts and words) are shaped by the things we believe. As always when it comes to sharing, it is worth coming up with an example or two beforehand to get things started.

### Bible Readings

This session covers four chapters of Joshua, which are full of hard-to-pronounce towns and cities. While it is worth encouraging the group to read through these chapters in their own time, the short section mentioned in brackets will suffice to give a flavour, while also bringing up the issue of the difficulties driving out the Canaanites.

### Key Verse

This is a great verse as you get a sense not only of Joshua's frustration that the Israelites haven't yet driven out the inhabitants, but there is also the certainty of God's promise – He has 'given' them the land.

### Discussion Starters

1.  While this discussion assumes the group have read the four chapters, it is fine to focus only on the passage in brackets.

2.  Although I have already answered this to some extent in the 'Opening Our Eyes' section, it is worth finding out if people have other ideas. Some may simply see the Israelites' failure as an inability to tackle a superior fighting force. If so, it's worth considering the earlier battles in the book, especially the one against the kings in the south, where God *clearly* fought for His people.

**3.** Paul's teaching that we are saved by grace and not by works is most clearly seen in Ephesians 2:4–9, which may be worth reading as the group tackle this discussion starter. Certainly, our salvation is only received through faith in Christ's finished work on the cross. However, as seen in the icebreaker, what we believe shapes how we live – our thoughts, words and actions – and so if we really believe that Christ died for the sins of the world and that we are the Father's children, called to serve Him through the Holy Spirit's constant guidance, this belief (aka faith) will be demonstrated by the way we live. Our actions, then, are the proof of our faith.

**5.** If you have time, it is worth reading each verse in turn and considering what promise it contains, and therefore how it might shape your thoughts, words and actions.

**6.** This may prove to be a controversial discussion starter, as some believe God's promises come to pass no matter what we do or believe. This was because the God had promised to drive out the Canaanites, yet it is clear from Scripture that this did not come to pass. This was because the Israelites failed to respond to God's word with faithful action.

**7.** As with the final discussion starter in the previous week, this could be tackled as a role-playing exercise. To help with the discussion, consider these six 'C's. Concentrate (take the time to listen). Compare with Scripture (the Holy Spirit will never contradict the message of love and grace as seen in Scripture). Conviction (His words often come with urgency and a desire to act). Counsel (for some things, it is worth seeking wise, godly counsel to help discern if the Holy Spirit is guiding you). Carry it out (if you believe He has spoken, act on it, through this you will also learn to discern if you have really heard

from Him). Commitment (learning to hear God's voice takes perseverance, but it's definitely worth it). This may present a good opportunity to pray for each other, to better discern the Holy Spirit's voice, or for specific guidance if required.

## Week Four: The gift of special cities

The Levites were spread throughout the land, scattered among the other tribal allotments. Their role was to teach the people about God, remind them of all He had done and said, and ensure godly justice was maintained. In much the same way, we are called to mix with others – Christians and those of other or no faith – demonstrating godliness and shining as His light.

### Opening Icebreaker
The aim of this icebreaker is to get the group to think about good things being spread around rather than being lumped together in one place. Some other examples could be: extensive farming, where animals have large spaces and different areas to live in, rather than being kept intensively, which promotes disease and lack of natural behaviour; rain falling across the land, which results in distribution of water for crops, animals, reservoirs and rivers, rather than in one place, which could lead to flooding and extreme erosion; and information, which used to be found in specific locations, such as the library or with experts, and is now spread across the internet, ready for people to access at any time.

### Key Verse
This verse simply states that the Levites were given 48 cities by the other tribes. It may be worth getting hold of a map of these cities, so the group can visualise just how spread out the Levites were. Six of these cities were 'cities of refuge'.

## Discussion Starters

**2.** In this famous passage from the Sermon on the Mount, Jesus teaches His followers not to worry about food and clothing – the basics of life, which by inference covers everything we need. Our role is to serve God and trust in His provision.

**3.** Although this is tackled in the 'Opening Our Eyes' section, it is worth taking the time to go through it again to see just how important the Levitical tribe were, and how similar their role was to our own as God's people today.

**4.** This discussion starter is not an easy one – thinking of examples may take some time, so it is worth getting the ball rolling by preparing an example or two beforehand. Bear in mind that the examples don't have to be from the group members' own experiences. They could use examples from Scripture, from Church history or even the secular world, and the simple feeling of pleasure derived from giving to those in need is a perfectly acceptable example.

**5.** The first part of this discussion has already been explored to a certain extent. When considering the second part, it is worth looking at what happened in the book of Judges, where we see that the Levites failed to teach the people about God and so, in a single generation, they forgot about Him and worshipped Baal and Asherah. Perhaps a more pertinent question is: What might have been the result of the Levites *succeeding* in their responsibility to teach their fellow Israelites and ensure the law was upheld? It might be worth mentioning the spreading of good things as considered in the icebreaker.

**6.** Try to avoid getting bogged down in every possible way that the use of salt might be compared to Christians (eg salt stops decay, it melts ice and it helps heal wounds). Jesus' fundamental point is that salt makes a difference, and so should His followers.

## **Week Five:** Conflict across the Jordan

This story of the tension between the tribes on either side of the Jordan is both sad and bizarre. It highlights the necessity for God's people to be united – avoiding gossip, slander and anything else that leads to conflict, while promoting understanding and good communication.

### Opening Icebreaker
Rebus puzzles can be found very easily on the internet. They are pictures that portray a common word or phrase. You could print a few off or show them on a tablet. The point of the icebreaker is that, when you work together as a team, problems tend to be solved more effectively than when tackling them alone.

### Key Verse
While this is actually two verses, it is a single sentence in both Hebrew and English, and it's where we find the Canaan-based Israelites spreading word about the new altar and deciding to start a civil war.

### Discussion Starters
**2.** Although this is covered in the 'Opening Our Eyes' section, Joshua's absence from the war council is such a staggering occurrence, it deserves further consideration. The full account of Phinehas's actions in Moab can be found in Numbers 25:7–13, and our passage isn't the only time he is mentioned in the context of Israelite conflict.

In Judges 20, when Benjamin is nearly wiped out by the other tribes, he is mentioned as being the high priest (v28).

**3.** As usual with discussion starters that involve sharing personal experiences, it is worth thinking of an example or two beforehand to help get things going. If the group can't think of anything (or at least anything that wouldn't be considered gossiping or ungracious), feel free to come up with examples from the Bible, Church history or other sources. The aim is to get the message across that what people say matters.

**4.** To illustrate how much the Bible condemns the use of the tongue to tear down others, you could look through the following verses (Psa. 52:1–4; Rom. 1:29–30; 2 Cor. 12:20; James 4:11; 1 Pet. 2:1). There are plenty of others besides! It may help the discussion to consider how those in the group who have been victims of gossip and slander felt.

**5.** The fact that people are stronger when they work together as a team (as hopefully demonstrated in the icebreaker) could be considered as one reason for unity being important. See also the 'Seeing Jesus in the Scriptures' for another reason.

**6.** It might be worth asking the group to come up with a definition of humility to ensure you are all on the same page. The issue of cultivating humility is important as we humans tend to have poor memories when it comes to our own shortcomings. It is worth mentioning that the primary purpose of fasting is to humble us before God, reminding ourselves of the reality that everything we need for life comes from Him.

7.  As with similar discussion starters, it may be worth splitting up the group and turning this into a role-playing exercise. Bear in mind that, since the response could be aimed at anyone, people need to avoid the use of jargon or assuming a knowledge of Christianity and the Bible. While it is worth taking into account that not everyone wants to do 'church' in exactly the same way, and so different expressions should be expected to develop naturally, it is important not to shy away from the fact many denominations and local churches are the result of splits over various issues.

It would be good to spend some time praying together for unity in your local church community and in the broader Church, if you have time.

## **Week Six:** The Canaanite problem

In the first of the Joshua's final addresses to the Israelites, he focuses on the Canaanite problem. God has commanded that they be wiped out, and if the Israelites fail, it will be their undoing. For us, the message is that we need to be careful about the influence others have on us and we have on them in return.

### Opening Icebreaker

This is a somewhat tenuous link to the topic, but the reason for playing a word association game is that if someone said 'love' it is unlikely that the word 'obedience' would be associated with it. And yet it is an important association in the Bible, and in our lives. Another link could be that the Israelites were instructed 'not to associate' with the Canaanites. Like I said: tenuous!

## Key Verse

In this verse, Joshua issues what seems like a superfluous command to a nation supposedly devoted to God – the people must not mix with the Canaanites or worship their gods. And yet, we see that they end up doing both.

## Discussion Starters

**1.** The following two factors may help with this discussion starter. First, worshipping God came with a lot of complicated rituals, eating restrictions and multiple sacrifices, all of which were very difficult to maintain. Baal worship would have been much simpler and less prescriptive. Second, the draw of superstition should not be underestimated. When there is tragedy (such as the death of loved one or the failure of crops), people will turn to anything for comfort and protection, and if something appears to work once, it's imagined power can be addictive.

**2.** If we define worship as assigning worth to something, so that we give it our time, attention and other resources, an idol is anything we consider worthy of such resources. As such, anything can become idols – families, jobs, hobbies, sports, church activities, food, drink, films, books, the pursuit of fame, money, beauty and so on. The only thing that cannot be an idol is God Himself! When tackling the second question in this discussion starter, it is worth considering what the draw is to idols, what they promise, what they provide and what may be addictive about them.

**3.** It may be worth considering the extremes in Christian interaction with the world. On the one hand, there is the monastic lifestyle – being cut off from the world and all its influence. On the other, so fully embracing the world that we are indistinguishable from anyone else.

Consider also how keeping an eternal perspective can help, understanding our part in God's grand narrative, so that, while it may hurt to keep ourselves from certain people, places or things, we understand the necessity and know it is worth it for God's sake and our own.

**4.** As this discussion involves sharing personal experiences that may be painful, it is worth thinking of an example to share to help the group get started. It would, of course, be good to focus on positive experiences, but negative experiences may provide a good opportunity for the group to pray for one another.

**5.** This is where the icebreaker could be mentioned, specifically the fact that love and obedience aren't commonly associated today. It may help to consider how a child who obeys his/her parents could be thought of as demonstrating love. Similarly, though maybe less appealing, the love of an obedient pet.

**6.** As this discussion starter is so closely linked with number 5, the two could be tackled together, or even swapped around. As usual with sharing experiences, it is worth having an example ready to get the ball rolling.

**7.** By issuing a command, the suggestion is that the person is capable of carrying out what is commanded. Is it possible to make yourself love God? Is it possible to make yourself love anyone? The link between love and obedience may help as the group consider this, as may considering how love is developed in an arranged marriage where the couple may not have even met before their wedding day.

## **Week Seven:** The Israelites make a choice

In this second and well-known speech to the Israelites, Joshua issues them with a choice: serve God or serve idols. This same choice faces us each day: will we serve God or will we serve ourselves?

### Opening Icebreaker
The aim of this icebreaker is to remind ourselves that we all make vows and resolutions, but we don't always keep them. Some barely even last a day! So, when we decide that we're going to serve God, let's be aware that it's not easy and will take a daily decision to do so (but it's the best decision we could make).

### Key Verse
I would suggest this is the key verse of the entire book, as Joshua confronts the Israelites with the choice of whether they will serve God.

### Discussion Starters
3. In the Leader's Notes for discussion starter 2 of the previous week, I suggested that 'worship' could be defined as assigning worth to something, so that we give it our time, attention and other resources. I defined it as such because the English word was originally something like 'worth-ship'. What might also help this discussion are the following Hebrew (first two) and Greek (second three) words: *shachah* (to bow down); *abad* (to work or serve); *sebo* (to revere or adore); *latreuo* (to serve); *proskuneo* (to bow down before).

4. It may be worth reading the 'Seeing Jesus in the Scriptures' section, which looks at Hebrews 12:1–2. Here we read that Jesus endured the pain and shame of the cross for the joy that was set before Him. It doesn't mean

we should enjoy pain and suffering, but in all service to God there is the joy of knowing that we are doing what is of most worth (see 1 Cor. 15:58) and it comes with a reward (see Col. 3:23–24).

**5.** Before the group meet together, take the time to think of an idol in your own life (whether current or in the past) and consider how it might ultimately be yourself you are worshipping rather than the idol. (For example, I have a weakness for television – it doesn't matter what's on, I'll happily sit in front of it for hours. The television is the idol, but really it is myself I am serving, because watching television offers me escape from my worries, it provides we with something to fill my brain with instead of the things I should be thinking about, and it gives me comfort. Me, me, me!)

**6.** One of the major differences between us and the Israelites is that they had the whole of the old covenant law to abide to, detailing what they could eat, wear, do and not do, together with hundreds of sacrifices and rituals. Paul points out in Romans 7:6 that 'we serve in the new way of the Spirit, and not in the old way of the written code'. Rather than trying to obey lots of impractical rules, we have the guidance of the Holy Spirit.

**7.** As with similar discussion starters, it may be worth splitting the group up and using this as a role-playing exercise with one person being the new believer and the other answering the question (then swap round). Remember that the role of the new believer is not passive – get into the role by asking questions that a person with little knowledge of Christianity and desire to learn might ask.

At the end of this week's session, it would be good to take the time to pray for one another, specifically that you remember the choice to serve God each morning, and that He would give you the strength and guidance you need for that service.

My prayer is that serving the Lord isn't something we once decided to do then forgot about like the Israelites, but that it becomes part of who we are as we constantly look to the Holy Spirit and respond to His prompting with faith-filled action. That is surely the best way to live.

# The *Cover to Cover* Bible Study Series

**1 Corinthians**
*Growing a Spirit-filled church*
ISBN: 978-1-85345-374-8

**2 Corinthians**
*Restoring harmony*
ISBN: 978-1-85345-551-3

**1,2,3 John**
*Walking in the truth*
ISBN: 978-1-78259-763-6

**1 Peter**
*Good reasons for hope*
ISBN: 978-1-78259-088-0

**2 Peter**
*Living in the light of God's
promises*
ISBN: 978-1-78259-403-1

**23rd Psalm**
*The Lord is my shepherd*
ISBN: 978-1-85345-449-3

**1 Timothy**
*Healthy churches – effective
Christians*
ISBN: 978-1-85345-291-8

**2 Timothy and Titus**
*Vital Christianity*
ISBN: 978-1-85345-338-0

**Abraham**
*Adventures of faith*
ISBN: 978-1-78259-089-7

**Acts 1-12**
*Church on the move*
ISBN: 978-1-85345-574-2

**Acts 13-28**
*To the ends of the earth*
ISBN: 978-1-85345-592-6

**Barnabas**
*Son of encouragement*
ISBN: 978-1-85345-911-5

**Bible Genres**
*Hearing what the Bible really says*
ISBN: 978-1-85345-987-0

**Daniel**
*Living boldly for God*
ISBN: 978-1-85345-986-3

**David**
*A man after God's own heart*
ISBN: 978-1-78259-444-4

**Ecclesiastes**
*Hard questions and spiritual
answers*
ISBN: 978-1-85345-371-7

**Elijah**
*A man and his God*
ISBN: 978-1-85345-575-9

**Elisha**
*A lesson in faithfulness*
ISBN: 978-1-78259-494-9

**Ephesians**
*Claiming your inheritance*
ISBN: 978-1-85345-229-1

**Esther**
*For such a time as this*
ISBN: 978-1-85345-511-7

**Ezekiel**
*A prophet for all times*
ISBN: 978-1-78259-836-7

**Fruit of the Spirit**
*Growing more like Jesus*
ISBN: 978-1-85345-375-5

**Galatians**
*Freedom in Christ*
ISBN: 978-1-85345-648-0

**Genesis 1-11**
*Foundations of reality*
ISBN: 978-1-85345-404-2

**Genesis 12-50**
*Founding fathers of faith*
ISBN: 978-1-78259-960-9

**God's Rescue Plan**
*Finding God's fingerprints on
human history*
ISBN: 978-1-85345-294-9

**Great Prayers of the Bible**
*Applying them to our lives tod*
ISBN: 978-1-85345-253-6

**Habakkuk**
*Choosing God's way*
ISBN: 978-1-78259-843-5

**Haggai**
*Motivating God's people*
ISBN: 978-1-78259-686-8

**Hebrews**
*Jesus – simply the best*
ISBN: 978-1-85345-337-3

**Isaiah 1-39**
*Prophet to the nations*
ISBN: 978-1-85345-510-0

**Isaiah 40-66**
*Prophet of restoration*
ISBN: 978-1-85345-550-6

**Jacob**
Taking hold of God's blessing
ISBN: 978-1-78259-685-1

**James**
Faith in action
ISBN: 978-1-85345-293-2

**Jeremiah**
The passionate prophet
ISBN: 978-1-85345-372-4

**Joel**
Getting real with God
ISBN: 978-1-78951-927-2

**John's Gospel**
Exploring the seven miraculous
signs
ISBN: 978-1-85345-295-6

**Jonah**
Rescued from the depths
ISBN: 978-1-78259-762-9

**Joseph**
The power of forgiveness and
reconciliation
ISBN: 978-1-85345-252-9

**Joshua 1-10**
Hand in hand with God
ISBN: 978-1-85345-542-7

**Joshua 11-24**
Called to service
ISBN: 978-1-78951-138-3

**Judges 1-8**
The spiral of faith
ISBN: 978-1-85345-681-7

**Judges 9-21**
Learning to live God's way
ISBN: 978-1-85345-910-8

**Luke**
A prescription for living
ISBN: 978-1-78259-270-9

**Mark**
Life as it is meant to be lived
ISBN: 978-1-85345-233-8

**Mary**
The mother of Jesus
ISBN: 978-1-78259-402-4

**Moses**
Face to face with God
ISBN: 978-1-85345-336-6

**Names of God**
Exploring the depths of God's
character
ISBN: 978-1-85345-680-0

**Nehemiah**
Principles for life
ISBN: 978-1-85345-335-9

**Parables**
Communicating God on earth
ISBN: 978-1-85345-340-3

**Philemon**
From slavery to freedom
ISBN: 978-1-85345-453-0

**Philippians**
Living for the sake of the
gospel
ISBN: 978-1-85345-421-9

**Prayers of Jesus**
Hearing His heartbeat
ISBN: 978-1-85345-647-3

**Proverbs**
Living a life of wisdom
ISBN: 978-1-85345-373-1

**Revelation 1-3**
Christ's call to the Church
ISBN: 978-1-85345-461-5

**Revelation 4-22**
The Lamb wins! Christ's final
victory
ISBN: 978-1-85345-411-0

**Rivers of Justice**
Responding to God's call to
righteousness today
ISBN: 978-1-85345-339-7

**Ruth**
Loving kindness in action
ISBN: 978-1-85345-231-4

**Song of Songs**
A celebration of love
ISBN: 978-1-78259-959-3

**The Armour of God**
Living in His strength
ISBN: 978-1-78259-583-0

**The Beatitudes**
Immersed in the grace
of Christ
ISBN: 978-1-78259-495-6

**The Creed**
Belief in action
ISBN: 978-1-78259-202-0

**The Divine Blueprint**
God's extraordinary power in
ordinary lives
ISBN: 978-1-85345-292-5

**The Holy Spirit**
Understanding and
experiencing Him
ISBN: 978-1-85345-254-3

**The Image of God**
His attributes and character
ISBN: 978-1-85345-228-4

**The Kingdom**
Studies from Matthew's Gospel
ISBN: 978-1-85345-251-2

**The Letter to the Colossians**
In Christ alone
ISBN: 978-1-855345-405-9

**The Letter to the Romans**
Good news for everyone
ISBN: 978-1-85345-250-5

**The Lord's Prayer**
Praying Jesus' way
ISBN: 978-1-85345-460-8

**The Prodigal Son**
Amazing grace
ISBN: 978-1-85345-412-7

**The Second Coming**
Living in the light of Jesus'
return
ISBN: 978-1-85345-422-6

**The Sermon on the Mount**
Life within the new covenant
ISBN: 978-1-85345-370-0

**Thessalonians**
Building Church in changing
times
ISBN: 978-1-78259-443-7

**The Ten Commandments**
Living God's Way
ISBN: 978-1-85345-593-3

**The Uniqueness of our Faith**
What makes Christianity
distinctive?
ISBN: 978-1-85345-232-1

For current prices or to order, visit **cwr.org.uk/shop**
Available online or from Christian bookshops.

# Be inspired by God.
## Every day.

**Confidently face life's challenges by equipping yourself daily with God's Word. There is something for everyone...**

### Every Day with Jesus

Selwyn Hughes' renowned writing is updated by Mick Brooks into these trusted and popular notes.

### Life Every Day

Jeff Lucas helps apply the Bible to daily life with his trademark humour and insight.

### Inspiring Women
### Every Day

Encouragement, uplifting scriptures and insightful daily thoughts for women.

### The Manual

Straight-talking guides to help men walk daily with God. Written by Carl Beech.

To find out more about all our daily Bible reading notes, or to take out a subscription, visit **cwr.org.uk/biblenotes** or call 01252 784700.
Also available in Christian bookshops.

 **Printed format**   **Large print format**  **Email format**   **Ebook format**

# SmallGroup central

**_All of our small group ideas and resources in one place_**

## Online:

**_smallgroupcentral.org.uk_**
is filled with free video teaching, tools, articles and a whole host of ideas.

## On the road:

A range of seminars themed for small groups can be brought to your local community. Contact us at **_hello@smallgroupcentral.org.uk_**

## In print:

Books, study guides and DVDs covering an extensive list of themes, Bible books and life issues.

Find out more at:
**_smallgroupcentral.org.uk_**

Courses and events

Waverley Abbey College

Publishing and media

Conference facilities

# Transforming lives

CWR's vision is to enable people to experience personal transformation through applying God's Word to their lives and relationships.

Our Bible-based training and resources help people around the world to:
- Grow in their walk with God
- Understand and apply Scripture to their lives
- Resource themselves and their church
- Develop pastoral care and counselling skills
- Train for leadership
- Strengthen relationships, marriage and family life and much more.

Our insightful writers provide daily Bible reading notes and other resources for all ages, and our experienced course designers and presenters have gained an international reputation for excellence and effectiveness.

CWR's Training and Conference Centre in Surrey, England, provides excellent facilities in an idyllic setting – ideal for both learning and spiritual refreshment.

**CWR** Applying God's Word
to everyday life and relationships

CWR, Waverley Abbey House,
Waverley Lane, Farnham,
Surrey GU9 8EP, UK

Telephone: **+44 (0)1252 784700**
Email: **info@cwr.org.uk**
Website: **cwr.org.uk**

Registered Charity No. 294387
Company Registration No. 1990308